Strategy
in a week

BOB NORTON
RAY IRVING

Hodder & Stoughton

A MEMBER OF THE HODDER HEADLINE GROUP

Orders: please contact Bookpoint Ltd, 130 Milton Park, Abingdon, Oxon
OX14 4SB.
Telephone: (44) 01235 827720, Fax: (44) 01235 400454. Lines are open from
9.00–6.00, Monday to Saturday, with a 24 hour message answering service.
Email address: orders@bookpoint.co.uk

British Library Cataloguing in Publication Data
A catalogue record for this title is available from The British Library

ISBN 0 340 849533

First published 1999
Impression number   10 9 8 7 6 5 4 3 2
Year   2007 2006 2005 2004 2003

Typeset by SX Composing DTP, Rayleigh, Essex.
Printed in Great Britain for Hodder & Stoughton Educational, a division of
Hodder Headline Plc, 338 Euston Road, London NW1 3BH. by
Cox & Wyman Ltd, Reading, Berkshire.

The leading organisation for professional management

As the champion of management, the Chartered Management Institute shapes and supports the managers of tomorrow. By sharing intelligent insights and setting standards in management development, the Institute helps to deliver results in a dynamic world.

Setting and raising standards

The Institute is a nationally accredited organisation, responsible for setting standards in management and recognising excellence through the award of professional qualifications.

Encouraging development, improving performance

The Institute has a vast range of development programmes, qualifications, information resources and career guidance to help managers and their organisations meet new challenges in a fast-changing environment.

Shaping opinion

With in-depth research and regular policy surveys of its 91,000 individual members and 520 corporate members, the Chartered Management Institute has a deep understanding of the key issues. Its view is informed, intelligent and respected.

For more information call 01536 204222 or visit www.managers.org.uk

CONTENTS

Strategy – what you do – and planning – how you do it, became amalgamated into strategic planning in the 1960s and 1970s. As businesses searched for more and more ways of achieving a lead over the competition, strategic planning became identified with models, mystery and mumbo jumbo as a preserve of the corporate planners, and very soon took on a life of its own.

In the topsy-turvy environment of the late 1980s and the 1990s, strategic planning failed to adapt and reinvent itself in the new business climate that was emerging, and failed to deliver its inherent promise: a future direction for the organisation.

Strategy in a Week separates strategy from planning, selects the best of the established methods, combines them with the new, and redefines what organisations have to tackle to create an effective strategy for the future.

Strategy in a Week traces the following developments:

Sunday	Introducing strategy
Monday	Strategic models
Tuesday	Strategists and strategies
Wednesday	Strategic analysis
Thursday	Strategic thinking
Friday	From strategy to action
Saturday	Formulating strategy

Introducing strategy

But there can be no fixed rules, for there are endless permutations, variations and surprises on the battlefield. As in the game of chess, one has to continuously profit from the varied experiences gained. Each confrontation with the enemy has in it lessons even for the most seasoned of warriors.

Reminiscences of an Ancient Strategist: the Mind of Sun Tzu, Foo Check Teck, Gower, 1997, p. 11

Traditional methods of developing strategy no longer 'fit' in the ever-changing environment in which organisations operate. There is a new approach to formulating strategy, and a new set of 'rules' has emerged which can mean the difference between success and failure.

Throughout this week, we will explore this new approach to strategy to understand how best to move forward in a business climate where the old rules no longer apply.

Today, we shall look at strategy by addressing a number of frequently asked questions:

- What is strategy?
- Why do we need strategy?
- What does strategy involve?
- What strategy isn't
- Where strategy fits

What is strategy?

There are many definitions of strategy, and the more there are, the more they tend to confuse rather than clarify. Most respectable dictionaries will tell us that the origins of the term 'strategy' are to be found in ancient Greek:

Strategia: generalship, command of an army

Stratos: an army

Agein: to lead

Strategy, therefore, has its origins in generalship and the art or science of conducting a military campaign or manoeuvring an army. The term 'strategy' entered business language only after the Second World War when military leaders on both sides of the Atlantic came together to see if some of the successful elements of waging war could be applied to business.

These origins help to clarify a question which continues to cause confusion in the business domain: is strategy *what we do*, or is it *how we do it*?

A return to military origins can help, this time with the Encyclopaedia Britannica:

Theory and conduct of strategy have traditionally been distinguished from tactics in the following ways: strategy deals with the entire theatre of war and the use of battles to win war, whereas tactics are concerned primarily with the use of troops and equipment to win battles, and the handling of troops on the battlefield.

In war, strategy deals with the overall formulation of campaigns prior to engagements on the battlefield. Tactics concern the actual manoeuvres, the specific actions to win the battle. Tactics are often called *sub-strategies* or *operational strategies*.

In football, the goal is victory by outscoring the opposing team. The game plan to achieve this goal is the strategy. The dead-ball free kick may be a tactic within the overall strategy.

Let us therefore establish our definition from the start:

> Strategy is about what we want to do, what we want our organisation to be and where we want it to go.

Tactics and planning are concerned with *how* we do things once we have decided *what* to do. Strategy and planning are not the same things: the former precedes the latter. This week, we address strategy.

Why do we need strategy?

The simple answer is that we cannot know where we are going without it.

All organisations get bogged down in routine tasks and the natural comfort of sticking to the way that things have always been done. This is because these have worked in the past. The ritual of simply trying to get things done can, however, make us forget exactly what we are trying to achieve and where we are trying to go.

Strategic thinking and change

If you take some time to consider the major changes that have taken place in your market over the last five years, would you have possibly been able to foresee them? Maybe yes, maybe no. Maybe some.

More importantly, though, ask yourself if, five years ago, you gave yourself the time to consider what the major changes would be over the next ten years. If you had, would your organisation now be in a better position?

Strategy provides an organisation with a framework for:

- understanding its position in the marketplace
- moving forward with a sense of direction, purpose and urgency
- focusing on the key issues of customers and markets, and on the skills needed to deliver to those customers and markets

A strategy should:

- make an organisation stand out from the competition
- make people sit up and take note
- capture the imagination and commitment of the workforce
- have a significant impact on the market

The only organisations that do not need a strategy are those which have no competitors, are in total control of their destiny, remain unaffected by changes in the marketplace, and occupy an environment that never changes.

Strategy, therefore, is essential for every organisation, large or small, public or private, service or manufacturing. On Tuesday, we shall look at some strategies that address – or are driven by – these factors.

What does strategy involve?

As we have said, strategy is about shaping the future. This involves addressing a number of questions:

1 Where are we now and how did we get here? What did we do well, or badly, to arrive at our current position?
2 What business are we in? Will this remain the same, or will we need to change our business? If so, to what? What factors internal and external to the organisation will, or can, have a telling impact on what we do in the future? These questions are principally about the first phase of formulating a strategy – strategic analysis – which we look at on Wednesday.
3 Where do we want to be in the future? We attempt to address this on Thursday when we look at what is involved in strategic thinking.

Only when we have addressed these questions, can we start tackling the question that has preoccupied planners for decades: how are we going to get there? Implementing a strategy is primarily about meeting the needs of the current or emerging market, which we look at on Friday.

The continuing strategic process
One criticism levelled at strategic planning is that the future is too uncertain for us to predict. Locking an organisation into a *plan* causes problems when things change. The problem now, as we know, is that the pace of change no longer allows us to plan 15, 10 or even 5 years ahead. The three questions raised above are no longer to be asked every two, three or five years, but continually. The strategic process we propose during the week attempts to build in flexibility and continuity to anticipate and embrace change, instead of fear it and respond reactively.

Strategy and time

In an age when old-fashioned strategic planning – involving a few of the senior elite closeting themselves away for the annual weekend – has been discredited, strategy is very much about making time for people to make a contribution. If you think that developing a strategy in this way is costly, then weigh up the costs of being caught unprepared for changes in the marketplace. We take a closer look at how strategic planning was dislodged from its pedestal on Monday, and look at finding the time for people to participate in the strategic process on Thursday.

What strategy isn't

One of the most well-known strategic bibles of the 1980s was *In Search Of Excellence* by Peters and Waterman. It had a significant impact on how people thought about the way organisations did things (even though many of the companies researched for the model of excellence fell from grace during the 1980s).

The excellence model encouraged organisations to examine concepts of quality and customer service and laid the foundation for many schemes – Total Quality Management (TQM), benchmarking, partnering, outsourcing, delayering and business process re-engineering (BPR) among them – which dominated corporate thinking in the 1980s and into the 1990s.

These schemes have produced operational improvements for the many organisations that adopted them. They all work, however, in the same direction, towards improving how things are done, cutting costs, and greater efficiencies in performing activities. As more organisations adopted them, so standards improved, raising quality for the customer..

If every organisation benchmarked for best practice, competitive advantage would ultimately be nullified because every organisation would be 'excellent' – performing similar activities very efficiently. But operational efficiency does not add up to business strategy.

- TQM can lead to improvements in operational efficiency but not a new strategic direction for the organisation
- BPR provides a process for reorganising how a company operates, but it won't – without some other source of inspiration and effort – galvanise management along a strategic path for the future.
- Benchmarking shows you how to catch up with the best today, but won't – on its own – create pioneers or new strategies.

We take a closer look at strategic models on Monday.

Where strategy fits

So where does strategy fit, and how does it relate to planning and managing change? Quite simply, strategy is at the top, and nothing can really start in earnest until the strategy is in place.

In business, strategy involves forming a path for the organisation to follow that will lead to products or services that customers will want. This will usually mean some kind of new departure for the business, requiring the leader to implement various tactics or sub-strategies. These tactics are usually set out in the component parts of the business plan.

So, strategy – and what you need to do to prepare the organisation before planning takes a hold – fits something like this.

Figure 1.

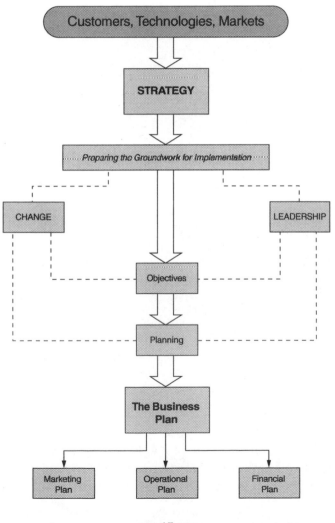

The business plan, a consequence of strategy, is the subject of a companion book in this series.

This week, we are concerned with formulating strategy and preparing the groundwork for its implementation. Principally, implementation is about how well leaders harness the resources at their disposal to start turning the strategy into reality. We look at preparing the strategy for action on Friday.

On Saturday we present a summary review of the strategy-formulation process, highlighting the key points and principles illustrated during the week.

Summary

A strategy needs to be:

- consistent so that staff and customers identify with what you are trying to deliver to them, but flexible so that the strategy can exploit change and adapt to it
- responsive to market and environmental conditions and not merely led by them
- imaginative so that it inspires commitment, but not so 'visionary' that it seems remote
- challenging so that it requires effort to attain, but realistic so that it may be achievable
- focused so that it is clear, defined and understandable to staff and customers, but not cast in stone

As all organisations are different, no two strategies are the same. We all have different strengths and weaknesses, we all spot different opportunities in different ways, and we all operate in different ways from one another. Strategies then will differ from one organisation to another, but the process of formulating strategy is similar for all.

Today we have attempted to distinguish the meaning of strategy from the process of planning and implementation. The 1970s and 1980s produced many models to facilitate the strategic process. We look at these models tomorrow and judge how applicable they are to the present day.

Strategic models

> *... each firm was working by trial and error, and all too often repeating the errors of others rather than learning from them.*
>
> *Management and Machiavelli*, Antony Jay,
> Hodder & Stoughton, 1967, p. 16

Today we look at various models designed to provide organisations with methods and systems for gaining advantage over the competition. We begin by asking where the models came from, and we conclude today by examining their legacy. We look at:

- where strategic models came from
- the models
- how the models worked
- what changed?
- why the models are no longer enough
- what the models don't tell you

Where strategic models came from

The concept of strategy was launched into a business world that was rebuilding and recovering after the Second World War. A long period of deprivation meant that consumer goods were hard to come by and choice was not on the shopping list.

It was a period when new technology meant heavy machinery to reduce the grind of factory-floor processes,

and when organisations grew in size, placing layers of
bureaucracy between those who set the tasks to be done and
those who did them. Inflation had no major significance for
business planning or budgeting, and markets were
relatively stable. What was produced was sold, and
consumers 'who had never had it so good' were largely
content with what was available, indeed to have it at all.

If there was one single catalyst for change which destroyed
the old order – but failed to replace it with a new – it was
probably the Oil Crisis of 1974. The hike in prices forced
companies and governments to rethink overnight as market
stability was shattered and organisations had to look for
new ways to achieve the same ends as before. In 1979
Margaret Thatcher launched the market economy on an
unsuspecting British workforce. The old rule book was
being torn up, and people searched for ways to start
compiling a new one. It was natural enough to turn to
systems or models to help impose or restore order when
there was little else to hang onto.

The models

Since the 1970s, models for formulating and implementing
business strategy have grown in type and number to tackle
the increasing complexity of the world around us.

We shall look at some of the major models which have
influenced the answers to the key question concerning how
to achieve competitive advantage:

> How can we beat (outperform, nullify) the competition
> to produce goods at a price that the customer will pay?

These models generate activities that set down a method for examining internal resources and external opportunities or threats in order to make logical proposals for the future. They concentrate heavily on planning *processes* and require extensive information gathering and manipulation. They enjoyed their heyday in the 1960s and 1970s as the numbers of people involved in data gathering, manipulation and analysis grew to provide the raw material for the planners.

The Growth Model

This model focuses on one particular issue: growing the market by reducing production costs and increasing sales opportunities. Growing the market could involve concentrating on a specific type of customer, product or geographic scale.

Today, however, success stories are quickly observed by market competitors. Copying the competition becomes an industry habit as technology and quickly formed

partnerships and alliances make market entrance affordable. It is hard to keep a growing market to yourself.

Porter's Five Forces Model
Michael Porter, in *Competitive Strategy*, argued that either you become the lowest-cost producer in your industry to achieve best performance or you differentiate your products in such ways as to attract customers at premium prices. In order to do this, the organisation has to select an approach towards *customers, suppliers, substitutes, competitors* and *new market entrants* depending on the industry conditions at the time: fragmented, emerging, mature, declining or global.

But it is not merely a question of collecting data in order to position the organisation favourably in relation to these forces. Porter argues that you have to break the rules and change them to bring the organisation competitive advantage:

- How can I reduce the influence of my customers and of my suppliers on my pricing?
- How can I limit the impact of substitutes – copies – on my product?
- How do I reduce rivalry in my industry, making competition unattractive, and nullify the impact of new industry entrants?

The logic of Porter's Five Forces Model has had a considerable impact on formulating strategy in the 1980s and 1990s. Such is the pace of industry and market change that companies now have to compete not just on one but on all five of Porter's forces. This process can be constrained by the amount of information gathering, analysis and interpretation that industry-, company- and market-watching require. We shall look further at Porter's Five Forces on Wednesday.

Growth by diversification/acquisition
Instead of going it alone, an organisation can buy success by acquiring another in order to gain entrance into new markets. Growth by diversification or acquisition gave rise to the formulation of analytical models that have enjoyed widespread application:

- The McKinsey/GE Matrix requires you to look closely at a company's market attractiveness in terms of its strategic position. It suggests acquisition and investment when an organisation is building a strong strategic position and market attractiveness is low. Divestment is recommended if the market becomes attractive to other players, and the organisation's competitive position is eroded.
- The Boston Consulting Group market growth/market share matrix became known as the Boston Box and attempted to indicate which businesses a company should invest in and which it should divest itself of. The model asks you to analyse which businesses have high market share and growth rates (Stars) and which are the opposites to these (Dogs). Moreover, if it has a high market share in a low-growth market, it is a Cash Cow which could yield significant, but short-term, gain; and the Question Marks are those businesses that have a low share in a high-growth market offering a questionable return on investment. See the diagram.

Figure 2. BCG market growth/market share matrix

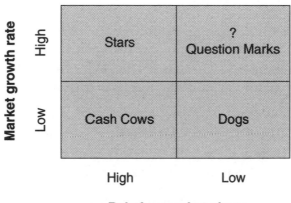

These models, and others, have proved useful for organisations wishing to diversify market risk. They still require, however, an accurate assessment of the prey's strengths and weaknesses, a good reading of which way the market will go and a probing estimate of the 'attractiveness' of the industry in which the prey operates.

Based on his Five Forces Model, Michael Porter established three critical questions to test whether an acquisition might be feasible:

1. *The attractiveness test*: is the industry 'attractive'? Is it one where there are only few rival products, competition is stable, and suppliers and customers have only moderate bargaining power?
2. *The cost-of-entry test*: is the cost of entry so high that a return on investment is at risk?

3. *The better-off test*: how can you demonstrate that either the acquirer or the acquired will gain competitive advantage from the link?

Growth by diversification means consistently monitoring the world outside the organisation. An equally vigilant eye has to be kept on the organisation's fitness for competition by looking at its own internal systems, processes and structure.

Porter's Value Chain
Porter's Value Chain focuses on the strengths and weaknesses at each stage of the supply chain to customers, and leads an organisation to examine what it is, and what it is not, good at.

The Value Chain looks at two different types of business activity: primary and secondary. Primary activities are mainly concerned with transforming raw materials into products and with delivery. These primary activities usually include:

- *inbound logistics*: materials handling, warehousing
- *operations*: turning raw materials into finished products
- *outbound logistics*: order processing and distribution
- *marketing and sales*: communication and pricing
- *service*: installation and after-sales.

Secondary activities support the primary ones and include:

- *procurement*: purchasing and supply
- *technology development*: know-how, procedures and skills
- *human resource management*: recruitment, appraisal, development and reward
- *firm infrastructure*: general management, quality, planning and finance.

To remain competitive and supply what customers want to buy, the organisation has to ensure that all these activities link together and fit, especially when some of them take place outside the organisation. A weakness in any part of the chain will affect the chain as a whole and impact negatively on competitiveness.

Core Competencies
The Model of Core Competencies, initially proposed by Gary Hamel and C. K. Prahalad, argues that an organisation can reach a position of competitiveness by analysing what it is that it does better than others. Looking at the organisation as a system of activities and building blocks – not as separate units of products and services – identifying core competencies means asking:

- How does activity X significantly improve the end product for the customer?
- Does activity X offer access to a range of applications and markets?
- What would happen to our competitiveness if we lost our strength in X?
- How difficult is it for others to imitate activity X and compete with us?

Success in core competencies means defining critical activities, and the skills that enable them, and investing in all of these to stretch and develop them.

Many organisations have not found this to be an easy process. And what happens if you get them wrong, or if the markets move away, or if you just hang onto them too long?

The McKinsey Seven-S Model
The Seven-S Model model suggests that the real value in an organisation is to be gained by looking at values other than the tangibles of capital, infrastructure and equipment. These 'softer' values are really about motivating the organisation's key resource – its people – to create a new competitive edge. The seven Ss are as shown in the diagram.

Figure 3.

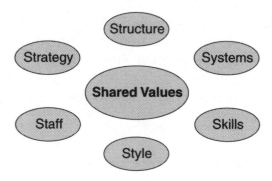

They laid the basis for the empowering style of management which Peters and Waterman, both working for McKinsey at the time, popularised in their book *In Search of Excellence*.

How the models worked

As the importance of strategic planning grew, its information systems grew to feed it. These consisted principally of Management Information Systems (MISs) and of Decision Support Systems (DSSs).

Management Information Systems

These were run largely by middle and junior managers and delivered large quantities of numerical data at regular times. The data was probably factually correct, quite well organised, but not too well analysed, and essentially historical. And because there was so much of it, managers used to spend large amounts of time looking for something salient. Eventually, they would come up with something predictable, gleaned tortuously from the computer print-out, or give up.

Decision Support Systems

These were based on the same data as the MIS above but were slightly higher-level in that they did permit some analysis that enabled the recipient to ask *What-if* questions. They delivered useful results on occasions, especially in the arena of spotting trends or patterns.

Because MISs and DSSs focused on historical data, managers' preoccupations were also influenced in that direction. Neither MISs nor DSSs could address the nature of strategic – future or directional – issues.

YEP – IT'S BEEN A
GOOD YEAR...
I THINK...?

The models and approaches above held muster when:

- forces driving society and business were relatively stable and predictable
- information gathered on past performance could be used with reliability for projecting the future
- strengths were not so easily copyable
- analysis of markets carried weight for some time into the future
- competition was either measurable or not a major problem.

In the later 1980s, confidence in these models of strategic planning fell and they were knocked off their pedestal. So what went wrong?

What changed?

In the 1970s and 1980s, the underlying business adage was: 'If it ain't broke, leave it alone'. The pedestal of strategic planning was lodged firmly in the upper echelons of the organisation, and planning – implementing strategy – was very much a top-down process. According to the formula, strategic planning was for the few to develop, for the middle to implement, and for the many to follow. It all started to go wrong when change speeded up.

In the 1980s, several factors led to organisational turmoil. The middle was knocked out of many organisations by cost cutting, outsourcing and downsizing. Others, small enough to be without much of a middle, found that their competitiveness was failing if they didn't adopt new working practices, such as empowering staff and using new technology. The world shrunk with more effective telecommunications, markets became global and cheap imports ate away previously secure market share. Market entry was made easier with a mobile workforce and new technology, and customers became more and more demanding as competition stimulated the thirst for something more and something different.

By 1990 – whether the organisation was small, medium or large – the rules of how to do business were changing faster than the ability to cope. This situation was further confused by the apparent conflict between key philosophies such as total quality and re-engineering – the former placing high value on people, the latter viewing them as disposable overheads.

To keep pace with volatility in the marketplace and gain competitive advantage, firms had to acquire new expertise, and reallocate resources on a grand scale in order to exploit new opportunities. Most of all, they had to innovate.

Strategic planning no longer fitted the way markets worked. By the 1990s, the adage was switching to: 'If it ain't broke, break it anyway and start again'.

Internet models

A number of internet models have been in evidence for some time:

1 *The Communication Model*: using the internet primarily for greater flexibility, efficiency and effectiveness through e-mail.
2 *The Advertising Model*: using the organisation's web-site as a shop window or marketing brochure.
3 *The Subscription Model*: offering unlimited access to a service in return for an annual sum.
4 *The Niche Marketing Model*: packaging personalised information, news, and perhaps, entertainment services. This model has grown into the *Community Model* where selected groups of people with common interests share them to the exclusion of others.
5 *The Department Store Model*: setting up as a seller on the Web. Customers can buy directly from the producer, lowering prices. New retailers emerge, bringing greater competition to the established market leaders with knock-on effects on pricing.

These scenarios paint alternative pictures of where the future may lie; adaptations and other alternatives are emerging all the time.

Why the models are no longer enough

The models still have a role to play in shaping our strategy but they don't give the whole picture. Models:

- can't predict the future with any certainty using information and experience from past conditions and circumstances – OK in times of stability but not in times of change;
- focus on products, markets and resources but not on generating values and capabilities for the future. What companies are good at today may not – and probably will not – be the critical success factors of tomorrow;
- become formulas for success concerned with maintaining the current position rather than frameworks for reflection, for questioning and for posing problems about where to go next;
- require an intensity of effort that locks the organisation into set processes and removes the flexibility to adapt and change direction.

What the models don't tell you

Models don't tell you about the unseen boundaries between organisations and the environments they work in, between management and staff, between planners and doers, between past and future, between those who formulate strategy and those who put it into action. Models don't tell you that they are neither formulas to follow slavishly nor frameworks to stimulate thinking. They don't tell you:

- not to turn strategy over to an 'elite' team of experts who have the monopoly on strategic expertise by dint of their position, but who, in fact, may be far removed from customer activities and the buzz of new developments
- that strategy may be led by those who have the greatest incentive for preserving the status quo, not changing it, for doing things the same, not for doing different things
- that something imposed from above, however well planned and justifiable, will not work as well as something built from shared ownership
- to question information and experience from the past instead of assuming its reliability and validity
- not to hold onto a strategy too long, when to drop it or change direction
- to do things differently and to do different things because it is difference that counts
- to experiment and try things out because nothing's for certain

Summary

Faced with a business environment where emerging technologies keep rewriting the rule book and markets grow and dissolve without consistency and predictability, we have to keep juggling several questions at the same time, questions such as:

- What is the organisation trying to achieve?
- What should it really be doing?
- Is there a difference between what it says and what it does?

Such is the pace of change, however, that these questions now have to be weighed not only against the organisation's resources and markets but also against new competition from outside its own industry.

By the mid-1990s, strategic planning as a discipline had lost its way because these questions had become too complex for the old models to provide a steer into an uncertain future. Just when organisations had lost confidence in strategic planning, new thinking emerged to turn much of the old on its head.

We look next at new approaches to strategy, bringing out some of the key points of the leading strategists, and some organisational strategies to illustrate them.

Strategists and strategies

The basis of such an approach is always to confront what is taken for granted in an industry or business with the simple question, Why? If, instead of accepting the first answer, one demands the reason for <u>that</u> and persists in asking 'Why?' four or five times in succession, one will certainly get to the guts of the issue, where fundamental bottlenecks and problems lie.

The Mind of the Strategist: the Art of Japanese Management, Kenichi Ohmae, McGraw-Hill, 1982

Today we are going take a look at strategists who have shaped the new wave of strategic thinking, and at examples of strategies from a variety of organisations. From this, we shall identify a number of key elements in the development of a successful strategy.

Strategy is a subject whose apparent complexity continues to fill endless numbers of books. The major writers on strategy, however, argue that there is no need for complexity, rather an understanding of some basic principles. These strategists are not just theorisers, but have taken some keen – and sometimes unpalatable – observations from companies which have succeeded in establishing strategies which work. Some key reading by each strategist is suggested for delving in deeper.

Today we look at:

- Strategists:
  - H. Igor Ansoff
  - Henry Mintzberg
  - Michael Porter
  - Gary Hamel
  - Ricardo Semler

- Strategies with:
  - grated cheese
  - telephones
  - children
  - crime
  - strawberries

H. Igor Ansoff

H. Igor Ansoff has been called the 'first great thinker of strategy'. His book *Corporate Strategy*, published in 1965, had a great influence on strategy and planning in the 1970s and 1980s. He put forward a complex set of rules that focused on undertaking a detailed environmental analysis that required innumerable processes and decisions.

Although Ansoff's approach was suited to the relatively stable business environment of the 1960s and 1970s, it nonetheless produced success for only a few companies, and confusion for many. It led, quite simply, to the production of more and more plans that never got implemented.

In *Implanting Strategic Management*, Ansoff looked again at his approach – which he recognised caused 'paralysis by analysis' – and redefined his methodology for developing strategy to include greater flexibility for the ever-changing environment. Under the term Strategic Management – a broader concept than strategic planning – Ansoff proposed his Strategic Success Paradigm, which holds that there is no universal success formula for all firms.

He concluded that turbulence in the business environment is *the* key factor driving strategy. A firm needs to align the aggressiveness of its strategy to the pace and extent of change in the environment, and to ensure that its management has the capability and competence to match those changing conditions.

Key text

Ansoff, H. I. and McDonnell, E. J. (1990) *Implanting Strategic Management*, 2nd edn, New York: Prentice Hall.

Henry Mintzberg

Mintzberg has often derided the role of strategic planning in the strategy development process, favouring instead an informal approach to the analysis of an environment in which an organisation operates. Analysing the environment too closely, he feels, leads to strategies that are simply copies of those of competitors.

Mintzberg distinguishes strategy from planning:

- Planning concerns breaking down a goal or set of intentions into steps for implementation.
- Strategy is about synthesising the broader issues in order to come to that set of intentions.
- Planning is about formalising the steps to achieve a goal.
- Strategic thinking involves creativity and intuition to form a longer-term perspective for the organisation.
- Strategy means reinventing new ways of attracting customers, not just reordering the accepted products and services of the past. This requires an energising, committing style of management to engage participants in the reinvention process.

Mintzberg believes that strategic thinking – the ability to identify change when it occurs, to identify discontinuities and to recognise opportunities – is the key to successful strategy. Too much emphasis is placed on the rational, calculating – planning – approach, when in reality, strategies are usually born of the prevailing, even imminent, environmental conditions.

Key reference

> Mintzberg, H. (1994) 'The fall and rise of strategic
> planning', *Harvard Business Review*, vol. 72 (1),
> pp. 107–114.

Michael Porter

Michael Porter played a leading role in the 1980s defining
the key elements of strategy with his research on
competitive advantage. In 2001, Porter addresses the
assertion that the internet renders strategy obsolete.
Although he admits that internet commerce is still in its
infancy, he can already observe that lack of strategy, in
favour of reliance on internet technologies to gain global
market penetration, is not proving to be a sound
approach.

He argues and illustrates persuasively that many internet
companies are competing by unsustainable, artificial
means, usually propped up by short-term capital
investment. He also argues that while the excitement of the
internet appeared to throw up new rules of competition,
the first wave of excitement is now clearly over, and the old
rules appear to be re-establishing themselves. Old rules
such as the 'Five Forces Model' (see p. 58), which are as
valid for internet businesses as they are for traditional ones.
And principles such as the basics of strategic positioning:

1 The right goal – healthy long-term return on investment.
2 Value – a company must offer a range of benefits which
   set it apart from the competition.
3 A company's value chain has to do things differently or

    do different things from rivals to reflect, produce and deliver that value.

4 Trade-offs – make conscious, deliberate sacrifices in some areas in order to excel, be unique even, in others.

5 Continuity – not only from a customer perspective but also in order to build and develop skills that bring a competitive edge.

Porter foresees that, as most businesses embrace the internet, it will become nullified as a source of advantage, and traditional strengths such as uniqueness, design and service relationships will re-emerge. For Porter, the next phase of internet evolution will be more holistic and involve the shift from e-business to business, from e-learning to learning, embracing an integrated mixed approach within which the internet will be a communications medium, and not necessarily a source of advantage.

Key reference

Porter, M. (2001) 'Strategy and the Internet', *Harvard Business Review*, vol 79 (3), pp. 63–79.

Gary Hamel

Read any of Gary Hamel's work and the word that stands out is 'revolution'. He believes that, to be successful in the modern organisational environment, strategy must not only be different from what has gone before but also be 'revolutionary'.

Hamel, like Mintzberg, argues that the strategic process has become too ritualistic, based on rules, and driven by the calendar. For strategy to be revolutionary, it must:

- be subversive by ignoring industry conventions, and aiming to be unique
- actively promote change, not simply be carried along with it
- let everyone have their voice, so that the new and young, as well as the tried and tested, are part of the process
- take risks, because we cannot predict the future with any certainty.

Hamel argues that it is usually senior managers who are the staunchest defenders of the status quo, that although they have the greatest experience, they also have the greatest investment in the past. He defines a new role for senior management which should:

- sponsor thinking about change and discontinuities
- consider all new ideas openly and honestly
- get involved in the learning process by casting off the mantle of omniscience
- foster intrapreneurship and participate in the creative process as team members, not just team leaders.

In 'Strategy, Innovation and the Quest for Value' (*Sloan Management Review*, Winter 1998, vol 39, no 2, p. 7–14), Hamel turns his revolutionary principles into action points and urges organisations to adopt a new stance, through:

- New voices – top management relinquishing its hold on strategy and introducing newcomers; young people and people from different groups bring richness and diversity to strategy formulation
- New conversations – the same people talking the same issues over and over again leads to sterility; new opportunities arise from juxtaposing formerly isolated people

- New passions – people will go for change when they can steer it and benefit from it
- New experiments – small, low-risk experiments can accelerate the organisation's learning and will indicate what may work and what may not.

Key reference

Hamel, G. (1996) 'Strategy as revolution', *Harvard Business Review*, vol. 74 (4), pp. 69–82.

Ricardo Semler

Semco, Ricardo Semler's $160 million Brazilian business, grows without a strategy and without plans. Semler says it is easy if you are willing to give up control and let your people lead you. Semco has grown from a manufacturing company to embrace property managment and e-business, not by careful strategy formulation, but by people taking the lead. '. . . give people the freedom to do what they want (a strategy in itself!), and over the long haul, their successes will far outnumber their failures.'

Semler's approach appears so revolutionary that business school lecturers claim he is too far ahead of current management practice for them to entertain disseminating his methods in the classroom.

Although Semler maintains he has no grand strategy, he would admit to having a number of operational, even tactical, principles:

1 Forget about the top-line – do not set financial targets for a business – let each find its own natural size.

2 Don't forget the start-up mentality – each business must justify its own continued existence and answer the question: what would we lose if we closed it down?
3 Don't treat employees like children – if you treat employees as immature, that is how they will behave.
4 Let people choose where they work – even choose their leaders. (Semco's turnover rate in the last six years has been less than 1 per cent).
5 Make decisions quickly and openly – the bureaucratic review and approval process kills initiative.
6 Partner promiscuously – a new business means a new alliance.
7 Stay free – build without fixed plans, without rules and control and without wielding power.

Key reference

'How we went digital without a strategy', *Harvard Business Review*, Sept–Oct, 2000, pp. 51–58.

Strategies

Now that we have had a look at the some of the thinkers on strategy, it is time to take a brief look at some strategies in action.

Strategy with grated cheese
Dairyborn found a niche market supplying ready-grated cheese to the catering industry, including Pizzaland and Perfect Pizza. This produced massive growth and success for Dairyborn. Then, its largest contract – Pizzaland – switched to a rival supplier. Dairyborn had identified an industry need and enjoyed dominant success, but it had no

strategy to face up to threat from a competitor. Two thirds of Dairyborn's business was lost overnight.

The options also became obvious overnight: drift or change. It took a step outside its established industry and went straight to the food manufacturers themselves.

Dairyborn is now successful again, this time through supplying cheese products to food manufacturers rather than the catering industry. The experience of losing the Pizzaland contract was instrumental in generating Dairyborn's strategy of differentiating itself from the competition.

Source: Bartram, P. (1998) 'The big cheese' *Director*, vol. 51 (6), January, pp. 32–36.

Strategy over the phone
Try to guess which organisation the following is describing and what service it is offering. It is taken from the organisation's promotional leaflet:

'_____ is the UK's leading 24 hour personal _____. Our personal service lets you take care of all your _____ needs by telephone, at a time and a place to suit you, 24 hours a day, 365 days a year.

Since the day we opened in 1989, we have never closed. Our friendly and professional _____ representatives are always on hand to assist you, which means that you never have to worry about catching us before closing time.'

First Direct at the end of the 1990s, was the most popular telephone banking service in the UK through innovative use of databases and automated telephone dialling, pushing back the boundaries of conventional service, and differentiating its services from those of the competition. This approach has made other banks wonder why they need their extensive – and expensive – high-street branch networks, and they begin to follow suit.

Strategy with children
Instead of tolerating a prevailing social trend on the part of youngsters to be disrespectful and disobedient, Horspath Primary School, Oxfordshire, turned this situation on its head and went in the opposite direction by setting up a value system based on respect and positive attitude.

The teachers believed that if they encouraged children to adopt respectful behaviour and attitude, there would emerge an improved platform for developing them in the classroom.

They involved the children in everything the school does, such as improving the school playground and establishing reward and discipline systems. Achievement stickers are awarded for politeness, punctuality and tidiness, and this transferred into the academic arena as well where teachers concentrate on the basics, 'the three 'Rs', whichever subject is being taught. A pupil is as likely to be reprimanded for poor grammar in geography or history lessons as they are in English lessons.

In 1997, Horspath Primary School was in the middle of the county school rankings; in 1998 it was ranked in the top 45 schools in the country.

Horspath achieved success by going against the grain, turning what is 'conventionally acceptable' upside down, pushing out the boundaries of standard teaching wisdom, involving everyone and demonstrating to children that they can influence their environment by learning how to be responsible for it.

Source: Harris, P. (1998). 'Ringing in the changes that spell success' *Daily Mail*, Tuesday, 27 January, p. 19.

Strategy with crime – NYPD

When William Bratton took on the role of Police Commissioner of New York, the city was a mess. Muggings, theft, assaults, burglaries and crimes of violence were all commonplace and people were leaving the city in droves in search of some kind of quality of life.

The rising wave of crime was accompanied not by public apathy but by inertia induced of fear and a lack of police will to stop the rot. It was better for the police to stay out of the way and keep their heads down: conventional wisdom

held that problems caused by society were impervious to police intervention.

Bratton, however, believed that the police could have a significant impact on crime, that the police could control behaviour on the streets. He decided to fly in the face of conventional wisdom by speaking straight to the police force, telling them that he needed their help to take the city back from the criminals, that he wanted them to be assertive, that he didn't want them to look the other way, that he wanted them to be honest and to forget the old 'rules'. And he said he would back them up. If they had problems, he would see to their retraining; if they were crooked, he would break them.

Bratton wanted to set targets to bring crime down by 10 per cent in year 1, 15 per cent in year 2, then 25 per cent after that. But he was faced with the prevailing view that already as much as possible was being done. There emerged, however, some support which indicated that progress and improvement were possible as long as *everything* was changed, in every police department, from top to bottom.

Bratton adopted a number of schemes to tackle guns, drugs, and quality of life, even squeegee people who threateningly smeared windscreens at traffic lights.

In his first 6-monthly figures in 1995, murder was down by 31 per cent over the same period in 1994; robberies were down 22 per cent, burglaries down 18 per cent. Bratton was hailed as the Enforcer, the Architect of Zero Tolerance. What he did was, in fact, to go in the opposite direction, tear up the old rule book which said what should and should not be done, empower and support his workforce, and apply the law. Strikingly simple when explained on paper, not so easy to do in practice, and highly effective when seen through to the end.

Bratton left NYPD after an apparent clash of interests with the Mayor, but two years after his departure, the city is still recording spectacular success in reducing crime. Brooklyn recorded a full week without a murder – the first since records began. And Bratton is still hailed as the Magician who cleaned up New York.

> Source: *Sunday Times News Review*, 22 March 1998, pp. 1–2, a review/extract from *Turnaround: How America's Top Cop Reversed the Crime Epidemic*, William Bratton, 1998.

Strategy with strawberries
The warmth of summer. The smell of ripe strawberries emerging from under their protective covering of leaves. The Pick Your Own sign attracts thousands to a pleasant ritual for a short season every July.

But is it really so pleasurable? The taste of strawberries is indisputable but many who pick their own also leave with aching legs, back and other assorted pains associated with uncomfortable bending and stooping.

Robert Symington of Seldom Seen Farm, Billesdon in Leicestershire has now changed all that for his customers. He has built a mile-stretch of homemade tables for his 2.5-acre site, which means that visitors can pick their strawberries at tabletop, or waste-height.

At present the tabletop technique can limit the crop to a few special brands, although the yield can be more prolific than at ground level. And there are extra benefits: 'tabling' enables a longer season as the berries ripen slower and later stretching the season for pickers into August. It also keeps the fruit safer from pests like mould.

Seldom Seen is the first strawberry farm in the East Midlands to experiment with tabling. The innovation has required an extra investment, but the strawberry-growers watch with interest to see if the results attract customers from further afield than usual, and how long it will be before others adopt the same practice.

Source: 'Tables enhance fruit quality' *Rutland Times*, 24 July 1998

Clairvoyance and diminishing returns
The mini-case studies above are not one-off, remarkable achievements accomplished by the lucky few – they are outcomes of customer focus, and changing the status quo to reflect better what the customer really wants (or, in the case of the NYPD account, what customers had coming to them!)

Great strategies are all around us. Take a look at the daily newspapers and it shouldn't take long to spot one or two. Why? Because they make news.

In the first edition of this book, published as long ago as 1999, we quoted the following household examples:

- Utility companies in the UK which have crossed industry boundaries to sell each others' goods – this trend has both consolidated and multiplied
- Flying Flowers, the Channel Islands-based home-delivery flower firm that can compete with the Interflora network
- Amazon Books, which enriches and diversifies the book-buying experience
- Cricket, where Kerry Packer transformed interest in the game with his one-day circus
- Snooker, which went from a seedy, back-room activity to an internationally televised sport

We also quoted the example of New Labour's transformation into the party of middle England.

Labour's grip on such heady heights was, at the beginning of 2002, no longer so sure with disenchantment ringing out from business as well as the press. Politics is not the only casualty in the new millennium. The dot.com bubble, the collapse of Enron, the stagnation of the Stock Market with its knock-on impacts all exemplify what we said on Monday – that models are not enough, that nothing's for certain and strategies can quickly get worn out, or simply not work out.

Hamel and Porter reveal the curious balance we need to embrace for successful strategies: a new approach which both breaks with the past (Hamel), but respects the tried and tested principles of strategic positioning (Porter).

The Common factors

When we look at successful strategies, we can pick out a number of common factors:

- being different
- learning from the past, but focusing on the future
- changing continually
- pushing back the boundaries of the industry
- being innovative
- involving people from all areas of an organisation in the strategy process
- developing a flexible, continuing strategy

We have already mentioned the term 'competition' many times this week. If we take a second glance at the strategies above, we see that the protagonists – particularly the school and the police department – moved beyond competition to create new values for the organisation and for those taking part in implementing the new strategy.

Now is a good time to reflect on what we've learned today:

> - Do you have a clear idea of what your strategy is?
> - How does your organisation or department develop its strategy?
> - Who is involved in the strategy process?
> - Does your organisation cling to its industry's conventions?
> - How different is your organisation from others in its area?
> - How-fast changing is the environment in which your organisation operates?
> - How different is your organisation today from two, five and ten years ago?

If the answers are unsettling, take heart from the cases above. Most organisations make mistakes, but the successful ones learn from them and change things.

Summary

Today we have looked at some writers on strategy, seen their ideas in practice and identified a number of key points in successful strategy.

For the next three days we are going to look at the key factors involved in developing a winning strategy. Tomorrow we will investigate the first of these: strategic analysis.

Strategic analysis

If your company comes to a plateau in earnings, take the time to look around and get your bearings. You may discover a whole new direction.

Up the Organization, Robert Townsend,
Michael Joseph, 1970, p. 198.

Today we are going to look at ways in which we can make sense of our ever-changing environment. We are going to look at some of the 'old' tools of strategy to kick-start the strategic process.

We will cover:

- What is strategic analysis?
- Looking at the environment
- Looking at our organisation
- Looking at the competition
- Change trends

What is strategic analysis?

Effective analysis is about asking the right questions. It is important to keep in mind that the inferences we draw from information related to the past and present are precisely that – past and present – and not automatically valid for the future. Too often, we superimpose the past onto the future, assuming that things will be the same, or at least similar.

Remembering Ansoff's 'paralysis by analysis', it is useful to try to discover how we got where we are, and to have a clear understanding of what we did well, or badly, and why. But it becomes counter-productive to linger too long on conundra from the past, and dangerous to project a mirror-image of the past into the future. If it is over-exercised, analysis can switch straight into planning without thinking through the factors which make the difference. The future is not what it used to be.

With that caveat in mind, strategic analysis involves taking a look at the environment in which we operate. This means looking at:

- the wider environment for significant influences, and picking out the change and discontinuity factors
- our organisation, and examining its strengths and weaknesses
- our competition, and assessing opportunities and threats

Looking at the environment

A glimpse back at the strategists we mentioned on Tuesday reminds us that we ignore the environment and its changing permutations at our peril. Some may take coals to Newcastle and some sell sand to the Arabs, but they are few and far between.

PEST analysis is a technique that allows us to look at our environment by dividing it into four categories – see the diagram:

Figure 4. PEST analysis

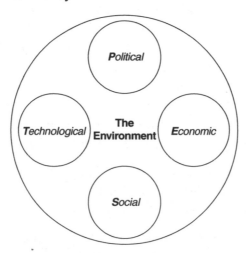

Here are some examples of PEST factors that have occurred in recent years, or are still continuing to roll out today:

- Political:
  - the shift towards capitalism and democracy in Eastern Europe
  - the recognition of the need to continuously 'read' the changing will of the people, instead of taking it for granted
  - moves towards Workfare in the USA and the UK

- Economic:
  - the opening up of new market potential in emerging economies
  - the departure of the UK from the European Exchange Rate Mechanism
  - the continued stance of the UK on EMU

- the impact of negative equity on the housing market – and other markets – in the UK
- a unified Germany
- Labour's handing over of the regulation of the UK interest rate to the Bank of England Monetary Policy Committee
- growing numbers of the elderly, and the impact of this on social security and pensions funding

- Social:
  - the growth of educated consumers seeking more choice, sophistication and differentiation
  - demographic shifts, with more women than men in the UK workforce
  - growing numbers of the elderly, and their impact on market forces
  - rising crime as an apparently 'socio-economic' phenomenon that we have to live with

- Technological:
  - the growth of the Internet and the advance of electronic communications
  - the affordability of computing in the home
  - the growth of cable and satellite TV and the service choices on offer

Looking at our organisation

One of the best techniques for taking a good hard look at the organisation is a SWOT analysis. SWOTs can apply across diverse management functions and activities, but are particularly appropriate to the early stages of formulating strategy.

Performing a SWOT analysis means gaining a clear picture of the Strengths, Weaknesses, Opportunities, and Threats which made the organisation what it is. Although the SWOT should keep to an organisational focus, it necessarily incorporates reflection on, and analysis of, individual tasks, activities, people, functions and processes.

It is customary for the analysis to take account of internal resources and capabilities (strengths and weaknesses) and factors external to the organisation (opportunities and threats). So, whereas PEST analysis looks at the environment in which we operate, SWOT analysis uses its findings to assess how well placed our organisation is. (See the diagram.)

Figure 5. SWOT analysis

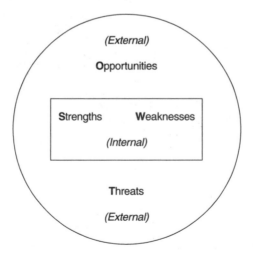

The effectiveness of SWOT as a means of analysis has recently been called into question because some of its practitioners:

- insist on the generation of long lists
- stop at description, instead of going on to analysis
- fail to prioritise

It is advisable to limit the exercise to the four or five most important factors affecting your organisation and focus thinking on whether these are really threats or opportunities (is the glass half empty or half full?). Do not concentrate on the marginal strengths or weaknesses of your organisation, but target the major areas.

Picking out strengths and weaknesses might go something like this:

Strengths	Weaknesses
Unique skills and competencies	Weak links in the Value Chain
Dominant product range	New product development drying up
Tradition of 'first to market'	Growth in staff turnover
Healthy balance sheet	Lack of 'spark' in the organisation
Creative teamworking	Growth of bureaucracy

As Peter Drucker said, asking the right questions is vital:

- What did we get right?
- What external factors enabled us to get it right at the time?
- What internal factors helped us to get it right?
- Are these factors likely to hold true in the future?
- What evidence do we have for suspecting this?

Looking at the competition

Michael Porter's 'Five Forces Model', that we referred to on Monday, can be used to identify the state of competition in an industry or market.

Figure 6.

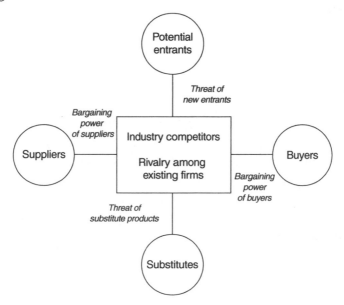

These five forces are:

1 *competitive rivalry*: competition is particularly strong when there are a large number of organisations competing in the same market solely on price and quality, and where differentiation between products and services is minimal.
E.g. the clothing market.
2 *the power of suppliers*: suppliers can reduce an organisation's profits through higher charges, and can be particularly powerful when there is a small number of suppliers and the cost of changing suppliers is high.
E.g. the 'old' utility industries in the UK.

3 *the power of buyers*: the power of buyers is increased when their number is small relative to the number of organisations within an industry. This force is inextricably linked to the following force below, i.e. the threat of substitutes.
E.g. the ready availability (supply) of cheap, frozen food (e.g. burgers, chickens) but relatively few large-scale outlets (buyers – e.g. MacDonalds, Asda, Safeway)

4 *the threat of substitutes*: if a buyer can easily obtain a different product that meets the same need as an existing product, then the threat of substitution is high and an organisation is unable to raise prices too high.
E.g. the advantages of e-mail over 'paper', although for many people the cost of switching to e-mail may make it sufficiently unattractive not to do so.

5 *the threat of potential entrants*: this covers the ease with which another company can gain entry into a market and so impact on an existing organisation. In some industries, the cost of entry in terms of capital requirements is so high as to deter potential entrants. In others, economies of scale prevent small operations from obtaining a foothold. Here, use of technology and temporary partnerships can rapidly change the shape of a market.
E.g. the move by supermarkets into banking in the UK.

Effective strategies aim to swing these forces in favour of the organisation. Porter's Five Forces Model highlights the importance of 'being different'. By differentiating our products and services, we can gain an advantage over the competition, but this differentiation must be maintained if competitors are not to catch up. Even so, this may still hold only marginal validity for the future.

Trends differentiating the future from the past

There are a number of general trends that we should be aware of:

1 *Globalisation.* Organisations, of any size, no longer operate only in their own locality. Nor do their competitors. Many organisations start up with the sole intention of operating world-wide; they have been called 'born globals'. If global sounds too ambitious, it is nonetheless increasingly important not to confine yourself to too limited a locale.

2 *Technological advancement* – particularly in the areas of communication and information transfer. The explosion of the Internet in recent years is changing how businesses operate.

3 *Societal change.* A profound shift has occurred in the West from a manufacturing-based society to the information and knowledge society; organisations are now competing on knowledge and information. Your competitive advantage depends on what you know and how you put your knowledge to use.

4 *The organisation as a collection of stakeholders.* It is now accepted that organisations are much more than a group of employees. Progressive organisations involve their suppliers, customers and shareholders, as well as their employees, in their strategy. These groups are the ones who have a 'stake' in the organisation, hence the term 'stakeholders'.

5 *The reliance on innovation for success.* Organisations that do 'the same old thing' while the environment around them changes are on course for failure. Innovation, doing new and different things, is what provides an

organisation with an advantage over its competitors. Tom Peters has coined the phrase 'Get innovative or get dead'!

6 *The nature of competition*. No longer do industry giants have an unchallenged monopoly. Small companies such as Netscape and Amazon Books can now compete directly with the major industry players.

7 *A more diverse workforce* – including older workers, women and those from ethnic minorities. Diversity both impacts on, and enriches, the working practices and services that organisations can offer.

8 *Changing organisational structure*. Where organisations use outsourcing, empowerment and communications technologies, they can be more flexible and responsive to market opportunities.

9 *The need for lifelong learning* – to ensure skills change with the requirements of the environment. It has been said that learning is the real key to competitive advantage in the future.

10 *The increasing speed of change* – and it's getting quicker.

Don't dwell in the past

Using your findings from brief PEST and SWOT analyses, and using Porter's Five Forces to find out the most important forces impacting on your organisation, try to address the following:

- What changes are happening in today's markets?
- In which market areas do you have the best chance of success?

- How are customers' attitudes and demands changing?
- Will the critical success factors of today hold good for tomorrow?
- How well do you think your organisation's current strategy will fit into the future?
- How quickly could your organisation change to take advantage of opportunities and defend against threats?
- Do you have the flexibility to change direction rapidly?
- How is technology changing what you do?
- What key skills do you need to develop?
- Do you have a learning workforce, or an obedient one?

Summary

Today we have taken a look at some tools that can enable us to identify the changes that are taking place in our environment and help to tackle the questions above. But analysis alone doesn't make a great strategy. We can recognise one when we see one, but how do we create one?

Tomorrow we look at strategic thinking.

Strategic thinking

> *If you want to build a ship, don't drum up people together to collect wood and don't assign them tasks of work, but rather teach them to long for the endless immensity of the sea.*
>
> Anon.

If strategic analysis is about where you have been in the past and how you have arrived at the present, it is not necessarily about how to take you into the future. Where the organisation is going in the future depends more on the capability for strategic thinking.

What is strategic thinking? How can the organisation create a climate where strategic thinking occurs naturally instead of being ignored, repressed or thought of as something that only others can do?

Today we shall look at:

- looking for something different
- what strategic thinking involves
- harnessing conflict
- getting involved
- finding time
- sharing information
- asking the right questions

Looking for something different

Continuous efforts to shave costs have resulted in increased efficiencies that have improved quality for the customer. In a period of intense competition, however, operational efficiencies alone are not enough. Strategy is about doing different things in different ways, about taking a different path from the mainstream, about standing out from the crowd. Cloning competitors' products works well when profits can be made from margins of improvement, but there comes a day when improvement runs out of steam because you have ultimately milked every improvement conceivable.

Looking for something different means making a case for continuous change because customers are always changing habits, preferences, needs and wants. As soon as you find them, they move on. Research and observation show that this is happening for the majority of customers over shorter periods of time and that the pace of change is speeding up all the time.

Looking for something different means going against the grain of convention – such as we saw on Tuesday – with strategies that break the mould. Doing different things means recognising what customers value, getting the customer involved to tailor and personalise products to stand out from the norm, and passing on visible benefits. It also means leading the customer to make discoveries and try things out. This is very much the case with products born of new technology: there was no great public outcry for mobile phones, for mouse-click technology or for CD-ROMs. There was, rather, a risk, along with intuitive foresight that this was where the market could go.

AND YOU'LL BE ABLE TO TALK TO PEOPLE HUNDREDS OF MILES AWAY.

Strategy can be based on method but it can also be emerging and dynamic. It can be adaptive but it can also be revolutionary. It can mean changing or developing products at the height of their success, before competitive watchers clone the product and eat away at market share. It means that imagination and creativity are given greater scope when it comes to trying things out.

What strategic thinking involves

Thinking strategically is not something you can turn on or off like a tap, nor is it something that can be set aside for an annual meeting. It is something that should take place continuously, perhaps in formal sessions, perhaps between individuals who have struck up a relationship which carries them outside the confines of day-to-day operations.

Strategic thinking is not just about solving problems. Problem-solving is related to norms and standards;

strategic thinking is about breaking the rules to write new ones. It is more about *creating* problems and setting challenges which take the organisation down a new path. Strategic thinking has a number of characteristics. It means:

1 casting off a risk-averse culture where things that are 'out of line' or not really 'our style' are not rejected out of hand or dismissed as the ramblings of a crank, but are positively assessed. It means allowing people to get things wrong and not always be 'held to account' when initiative or inspiration do not immediately meet bottom-line requirements;

2 being able to kick around ideas in a climate where colleagues and others have the freedom to explore new ideas, and where omniscience at the top is replaced with a recognition that no one individual or set of individuals can know it all. This means information sharing and communication on a different scale from the past. It means encouraging cross-functional conversations to get dialogue going in place of linear thinking which 'departments' and partitions tend to foster;

3 recognising that the same old voices will probably come up with the same old thinking, that those voices were once fresh and new, and now the strategic process needs invigorating again with new voices – the young, customers, potential customers and suppliers with a different perspective;

4 releasing some desires and passions to make that difference happen, and that means letting the patterns and rhythms of the right brain have their say along with the logic, order and calculation of the left. Research has shown that the left side of the brain is good at analysing,

using reason and putting ideas into words, while the right, on the other hand, is the more creative, intuitive side that sees the 'whole' picture;

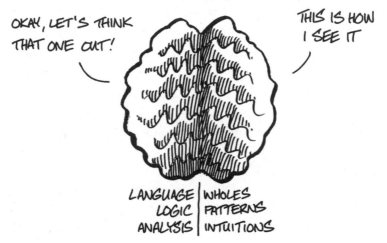

OKAY, LET'S THINK THAT ONE OUT!

THIS IS HOW I SEE IT

LANGUAGE | WHOLES
LOGIC | PATTERNS
ANALYSIS | INTUITIONS

5 nurturing creativity and new patterns of thinking through techniques of brainstorming, where people become involved in spontaneous, open-ended discussions in search of new ideas;

6 challenging old assumptions and suspending the judgement that new ideas don't appear to fit. Looking for new ideas means breaking away from the old 'fit'. This is very much akin to Edward de Bono's lateral thinking which is *concerned with breaking out of the concept prisons of old ideas. This leads to changes in attitude and approach; to looking in a different way at things which have always been looked at in the same way. Liberation from old ideas and stimulation of new ones are twin aspects of lateral thinking.*

Lateral Thinking: a Textbook of Creativity,
Edward de Bono, Ward Lock Educational, 1970, p. 11.

7   assimilating the notion that individual learning and
    development are at the heart of strategy, and that this
    may mean that the organisation reinvents its approach to
    individuals, how they are 'expected' to 'behave', how they
    manage their time, even how they are rewarded;
8   trying out new things. But that means conflict because
    some people will always prefer to stay with the way
    things are.

Harnessing conflict

Creating a climate conducive to the exchange of ideas and
the sharing of information means building relationships
which are founded on mutual respect, empathy and trust,
rather than on position, status and authority. It means
taking time to get involved in conversations and listening
to what others have to say instead of wishing to dominate.

We have learned that the way to manage interpersonal
conflict is to listen, treat the problem with respect, withhold
opinions and 'solutions' and get people to come up with
their own. Factors to be avoided include:

- the notion of knowledge as a privilege of position – the
  days when only certain individuals have the monopoly on
  intelligence, expertise and vision are long gone; now
  they are to manage it, nurture it, harness it and exploit it
  instead of own it by dint of seniority;
- ignoring undercurrents or sweeping differences under the
  carpet so that you can carry on as before;
- ignoring 'off the wall' contributions, which are, in fact, all
  the more valuable because they are different and require
  alternative treatment. Much 'blue sky' conversation may

happen, perhaps, but it is often dismissed as idle rambling or the outpouring of tacit rebellion;
- taking a shorter-term view of things 'that don't gel':
  - of compromise and conciliation that lock you back into the status quo
  - of paradoxes and contradictions that rattle against the norm
  - of organisational protection and face-saving that will probably see you keep on making the same old mistakes in the future;
- short-term projects which may seem exciting on the surface but actually divert attention from longer-term goals.

Getting involved

So how does real involvement happen? Not just token consultation when minds are already made up, positions are being defended, and change is viewed as a threat – not a challenge to keep the organisation ticking. There are a number of ways to build a climate of involvement:

1 Getting out of the office and walking about to build contacts and relationships and to find out what is really going on – not just what the monthly reports tell you – is important.
2 Some organisations have found that strategic away-days or weekend retreats *do* work. But they have to include a mix of key stakeholders – not just the corporate planning team. Participants go along to listen with openness and honesty, and to exchange thoughts and ideas which some might find uncomfortable. Making people uncomfortable is central when change is overdue. Some

parts of the organisation may have to recognise that what they thought they do so well may not be quite the view held by others.

3 Getting involved means *making* suggestion schemes work by planning out what will happen in terms of reward and feedback to the suggester, rather than just placing a box in Reception and flipping through it once a quarter. Strategic thinking means getting others involved by spreading strategy wide, inside and outside the organisation.

4 On an individual basis, it means making teams work, not by drawing people together from different departments or functions and giving them something extra to do – the 'project' – but rather by understanding what each can contribute towards shared goals.

5 It means understanding the basis for trust in the organisation. Trust works OK when individuals begin to rely on each other in a continuing working context, but when they only meet now and again, it is not so easy. In some cultures, trust can hinge on a person's dependability to deliver on promises and meet deadlines; in others, renegotiating timetables is not seen as critical. In some cultures, a pervasive air of disagreement and suspicion leads people to get hung up on minor points and become entrenched in fixed positions; in others, respect and sincerity are enhanced by 'straight talk' and eye-to-eye contact. In others again, direct eye contact is an indicator of anger or aggression.

6 Getting people involved also means taking time to let them feel their way. It may be time-consuming at the beginning, but it is better to start slowly, in tune with the adaptability of those concerned, rather than blow things apart by going too fast.

Finding time

So how do we bring about these changes to the way we work in order to create 'thinking' time?

Unfortunately, there are no magic formulas for time management. Most of us are relatively poor at self-discipline and dominated by day-to-day problems that send us crashing from one interruption to another, forgetting what is important and driven by the urgent. The confusion between the urgent and the important can create conflicts for the individual. But it is the urgent which envelops us in firefighting and problem-solving because things have to be 'put right' before all else. When the urgent dominates, it also tends to reinforce the status quo.

How often do we set aside time for:

- planning development activities
- coaching and counselling colleagues
- building relationships
- getting honest feedback on the way we work
- concentrating on self-development
- taking time out to read or explore pastures anew?

These are activities – we say – which are important, but we tend to postpone them, push them back, or carry them out far too infrequently. Yet these are the *very activities which can change the way we work*. Changing priorities is not about cramming more into an overcrowded day; it is more about making a strategic reassessment of what can really help to change the focus of the workplace, and getting to grips with activities which are too often postponed.

Sharing information

Information and knowledge sharing is now recognised to be the key factor in an organisation's efforts to compete in the marketplace. Creativity – the ability to come up with ideas that work – is *the* asset which has distinguished the rule makers from the followers.

Successful organisations have moved away from the past when information meant personal power. Information hoarders have been bypassed by open systems of communication such as Intranets which become the first and last resort for depositing and finding information within the organisation.

Sharing ideas, keeping others abreast of progress, projects and developments, making information available to those who might pick it up and run with it are all seen as key components of the organisation's developing as a knowledge organism.

Asking the right questions

Asking the right questions means getting down to a thorough health check of the *key factors* you have to get right if you are to cope with strategic change:

- *Strategy*: does everyone know what they are doing and why? Do they know how they contribute to the strategic objectives of the organisation?
- *Leadership*: does the leader set an example, act as a role model and foster learning and development?
- *Customers*: does everyone have a good understanding of their needs and expectations? Are we going to try to steer them, outguess them or just hope for the best?
- *People*: are our people developing, innovative and responsible? Do people think naturally about what's coming next? Or will the next change be met with the same old shock and horror?
- *Control*: do measurement and procedural control stifle creativity?
- *Integration*: do we have a business of people in separate boxes or do we mix across areas, functions and responsibilities?
- *Processes*: which are the key activities and processes which give us our strength?
- *Results*: is our focus entirely on the short-term bottom line, or are we looking 3–5 years ahead and investing for it?

Asking the right questions also means getting the imagination to work on the key strategic drivers that affect the way the marketplace works. It can often mean leading customers rather than following them. Focusing on the future does not mean forecasting, predicting or working out a plan – usually, such attempts end in ignominy. It does, however, mean accepting that change will probably take us all onto a new playing field.

Strategy today means tackling the questions that will shape a tomorrow where, sooner or later, perhaps:

- over 90 per cent of homes are linked up to the Internet and/or Cable TV
- cyber-homes look after their residents, with one computer controlling lighting, security, heating and appliances, and righting malfunctions while another provides online banking, shopping, recreation and education services

- businesses operate 24-hour services as a norm through virtual link-ups and call-centres
- fossil fuels have become so expensive that there are fewer cars on the road than in the 1950s
- climate changes have shifted the Gulf Stream to create hotter summers but colder winters in Northern Europe

Blue-sky perhaps, but strategically these pictures – or others – of the future will shape what business is done and how.

If one key to competitive advantage means being first, then we need to take the simple questions and project them three, five years forward:

- Who will be our customers in the future?
- What will be their concerns and priorities?
- What kind of lifestyle will they have or expect?
- How shall we get close to them?
- What will be customer preferences for getting access to products and services?
- What will be the major channels for reaching customers?
- How can we adapt or radically transform our products and services for future requirements?
- What should we do to exploit information, develop knowledge and invest in skills?

Summary

Today we have looked at some of the factors involved in strategic thinking, which can break us away from the mould of conventional routine and attitude. Tomorrow we look at how to take this forward by turning the strategy in development into action.

Towards a new strategic model

If the old models are defunct – at least as self-sufficient competitive weapons – and the concepts we described yesterday are at the heart of organisational development, what can we postulate as something of value, something more than a fad, something that may act as a basis for a new strategic model?

> '. . . in the not too distant future, it may be only the learning organisations that survive and prosper.'
>
> Peter Senge

Today we shall look at:

- what the new model needs to incorporate
- making change work
- towards a new strategic framework
- organisational tools for the job
- making learning work for the individual
- drawing up the learning strategy

What the new model needs to incorporate

1 The harnessing of organisational knowledge
There has been much fruitless debate on what comprises knowledge. Unless the organisation starts to become aware of what it knows and what it doesn't, then it cannot hope to innovate or penetrate new markets, except perhaps by serendipity.

2 The potential for creativity and innovation
It is individuals who come up with ideas, and organisations that have the resources to turn those ideas into innovations.

Shifting, however, from a 'follower' organisation to an innovative one – where Thursday's notions happen naturally – is not easy. There are several core competencies and behaviours that support innovation, such as a widespread organisational capacity for:

- tolerating failure, showing support and a focus on learning
- a high regard for individuals
- a willingness to alter targets
- real, not rhetorical, openness and honesty
- individuals' development linked to clear organisational goals
- balancing risk with progress

If such competencies and behaviours are not in place, rhetoric gives rise to an all too familiar reality where, as Morgan and Maddock point out (*Core Conflicts in Managing Change*, 2000):

- innovation is promoted . . . but risk-takers are sidelined or ignored, perhaps even punished
- quality is promoted . . . but it is quantity that is measured and rewarded
- strategy is discussed . . . but management is reactive and focuses on operational issues
- flexibility is espoused . . . but time-keeping and 'face-time' are practised
- training is valued . . . but is still a box to be ticked
- openness is lauded . . . but realities are still kept hidden, or ignored

This situation has much to do with the organisation's leadership and the willingness to adopt Thursday's concepts. If the organisation does not take on these ideas, then although a willingness for innovation may be expressed, it is likely to materialise over time that general energy and interest in innovation gradually disappear.

3 The mix of old and new technologies

Something that jargon grinders have labelled as clicks and mortar. Experience has shown so far that purely Web-based services have yet to show sustainable competitive advantage. Similarly, current wisdom holds that any organisation ignoring the Web, is deliberately shooting itself in the foot. Getting the mix right, so that electronic ease and convenience are combined with the human touch of relationship building, is an approach which seeks to exploit the best of both worlds and not sacrifice one for the other.

4 Leadership learns, listens and grows the organisation

Henry Miller once said that the real leader has no need to lead – he is content, rather, to point the way. It is an insight taken up by managmenet guru Henry Mintzberg who describes Ricardo Semler's leadership approach as one which manifests *'the brilliance of knowing when to lay off'*. Mintzberg claims that the best kind of leaders are like queen bees. While they keep everything together at the centre, it is the other bees who explore the outside world, return with sustenance and keep the hive alive in the face of the changing environment.

5 Evolution versus revolution

When organisations become stagnant they do need a revolution to shake them out of the doldrums. Many of late 20th-century leaders – Jack Welch, Andy Grove, Phil Knight and Ricardo Semler – who have entered the hall of fame have done just that. But revolution is unsustainable in the longer term – it needs to settle into something evolving and developmental so that change and adaptiveness become in-built and continuous.

Making change happen

One route towards making change and learning a reality in the organisation has been proposed by Richard Pascale who uses the words 'transformation', 'revitalisation' and 'reinvention' when he talks of strategy.

He proposes that organisations have to harness themselves to perpetual change in order to be successful. It is important, he advises, that organisations should not merely seek improvement but also create something that *isn't already there*. In other words, they must become a totally different company again and again (see the Semler case study on Tuesday).

The path to reinvention requires a mix of so many competencies and behaviours that it is not possible, let alone desirable, to rely solely on senior management. The burden of change must be placed on all of the organisation's employees if it is to succeed, not by mere imposition but by argument, persuasion, convincing, listening and by securing co-operation.

For Pascale, there are four vital indicators of an organisation's fitness for adaptability and strategic change:

1 *Power*: do employees believe that they have the power to make things happen? If not we return to the dismal innovation failure loop.

2 *Identity*: do employees narrowly identify with their own section or unit, or with the organisation as a whole? Are employees encouraged to see the bigger picture? Do they understand how success or failure in one unit may impact on them all?

3 *Conflict*: do employees try to smooth over conflicts to safeguard the status quo, or do they try to confront and resolve them? Back to Semler: '*Every time we abort a conflict, we are aborting the chance to solve it*' ('Chief Destruction Officer', *Human Resources*, Jan 2001).

4 *Learning*: how does the organisation handle new ideas? Refer back to Thursday.

Towards a new strategic framework

In developing an organisational learning strategy, therefore, a major objective outcome is to be able to develop new value on a continuing basis. In order to do this, the organisation must establish processes which are designed to improve the way things are done. To do that there must be the capability to try out new things or new ways in a spirit where learning, not failure, will be a major recognition. To do that, there has to be processes in place to help, train and develop those who need it. Similarly those who wish to explore must be allowed to do so (within certain agreed boundaries such as budgets, time-scales and organisational goals).

In order to tackle these requirements the organisation needs tools which get to grips with:

- the strengths and weaknesses of its current knowledge and learning processes
- industry trends, individuals' ideas and potential for creativity
- that which is regarded as best practice in the field

Organisational tools for the job

For an organisational learning strategy to work, the organisation will need to build, access or buy tools which help to:

- paint an accurate picture of the current organisational profile
- analyse strengths and weaknesses
- exploit best practice

1 Paint an accurate picture of the current organisational profile
The organisation needs to assess and face up to exactly where it stands in terms of the current learning level of its employees. This is not done by merely counting days spent on training courses. At best these are inputs, at worst they are empty statistics. Much better to examine what employees, learn, how they learn it and, most importantly, how they apply it in the workplace. Such tools need to address classic information audit questions such as:

- What information do employees acquire? How is it used? What happens to it?
- What information do staff create? How is it used? What happens to it?

- Where is it stored? Who has access to it? How often is it used? What for?
- Is it updated, renewed, revised, ignored?
- How is it applied in the workplace? What purpose does it serve?
- What indicators do we have to show that these processes are productive/creative?
- Do any of these information processes lead to new ideas?
- What happens to the new ideas?
- Do we have a process for examining new ideas and turning them into reality?
- Do we know how many ideas we have coming through?
- Do we know how many are tested and rejected, or accepted and converted into innovations?
- Do we know why and how they are rejected?
- Do we know why and how they are accepted?
- Do we have ready access to acceptance/rejection criteria?
- Are new ideas on the increase or decrease?
- Why?

2 Analyse strengths and weaknesses
A ready-made tool which can be exploited on a continuous basis for examining and assessing the organisation's strengths (weaknesses) and opportunities (threats) can offer the organisation a vital perspective if it is kept up to date, renewed and revised on a regular basis. Look back to Wednesday for another glimpse at what the SWOT and PEST analyses can offer, and then imagine those tools converted into software that evaluates and assesses strengths and weaknesses, analyses the data and converts it into opportunities or threats scenarios.

3 Exploit best practice

There are a number of ways that you can decide on an appropriate learning strategy. One is to try things out and work them through, if you have the time. Another is to exploit best practice. This latter is arguably faster and will sharpen the learning curve. Why reinvent the wheel? Why not take the best that is going, then convert it into the shape you need for your culture, your style, your competencies and behaviours and your application? Like the very best of wines – so they say – best practice rarely travels from A to B without some adaptation. But even then, the best wines still taste a lot better than cheap plonk.

If the organisational profile and the SWOT have been completed, that analysis can be matched against best practice processes and studies for a learning strategy to emerge.

Making learning work for the individual

Organisational learning initiatives and tools must, if they are to be effective, cascade down into individual skills, behaviours and competencies. It is a truism to argue that organisations don't learn, people do. It is more salient to assert that if their people do not learn then organisations won't. So how can organisational initiatives spin down into action for the individual?

Some people learn naturally on the job and some jobs are natural learning mechanisms for their incumbents.

To be realistic, however, the current picture may not be all that encouraging. There are three approaches to employee learning which may do little more than pay lip service:

1 *Rhetoric*: most of us are familiar with high-sounding even well-meaning, but empty phrases, advocating what some would like to believe are in place, without making it happen. The outcomes fit the failure criteria outlined earlier today.

2 *Training days*: most people associate learning – and hopefully its subsequent development – with training days. This is not to denigrate the hundreds of thousands of days people spend in classrooms every year, but training provides input – it does not ensure that the employee takes the learning on board or even that the employee *can* take the learning on board. Training ensures a break from routine, exposes the participant to something new, or confirms existing practice. It does not ensure learning, although it helps. But more often than not, it takes no account of the ways that people learn or of each individual preferred learning style.

3 *CPD*: acronym for Continuing Professional Development. CPD is an all-embracing term for keeping up to date, learning new skills and avoiding obsolescence in the job. CPD schemes have been around for a long time, on a formal or informal basis. With greater instability in the employment market, brought about by massive changes to working practice in the last 10–20 years, CPD has been seen as the key to employability. Update your skills, learn new ones and this will do as much as is feasibly possible to enable you to find jobs. Makes sense. The problem is that most CPD schemes stop with training time and they generally measure inputs, not developments and outcomes which can benefit the organisation. This is now changing.

As an individual application of organisational learning initiatives, CPD schemes are now emerging which help you to assess your general and specific skills, give you feedback and signposts to learning opportunities and, more importantly, assess how you are learning and how you apply that learning in the workplace.

Such a scheme has recently been launched by the Chartered Management Institute. This has a number of individual learning tools which can 'fit' the organisational tools outlined above.

The IM scheme is built around two learning tools:

1 *Smart Management Assessment*: a questionnaire that investigates your ability across general management areas – managing people, managing operations, managing resources, managing information and managing yourself. The scheme scores how you rate yourself in each area and provides feedback on those areas, offering practical learning and development advice. This tool is the individual equivalent of the organisational profile and SWOT.

2 *Smart Skills Benchmarks*: a series of diagnostic tools covering a wide range of management skills, from managing your time to handling stress, from your ability to influence to your ability to manage projects. These tools provide you with feedback on your own assessment and invite you to ask others to assess you, thereby enabling a broader 360º perspective. They also signpost a wide range of learning opportunities. These are the individual equivalent of an organisational SWOT and search for best practice.

And one assessment tool:

- *Smart Learning Assessment:* a tool which examines your learning, your application of new skills in the workplace, your working behaviours and any outcome or impact in the workplace.

The Institute scheme starts to bridge the formerly enormous gap between individual learning and organisational development, with indicators, measures and a route map.

Drawing up the learning strategy

So how does all this fit together in an organisational learning strategy designed to embrace change and incorporate learning and development to bring new value to the organisation? The emerging learning strategy model looks something like figure 7, on the next page.

Summary

In the past, differences between individual and organisational values have been pinpointed as one of the reasons for lack of cohesive progress and development. Today we have looked at ways of drawing up an organisational learning strategy and shown ways in which the concerns of the individual may be integrated – assuming that employability is a major concern for the individual.

Tomorrow we bring together many of the themes covered in the week and summarise the key factors for formulating strategy.

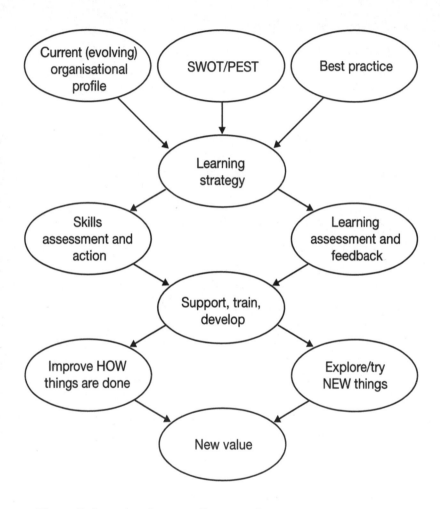

Figure 7. Learning Strategy Framework

Formulating strategy

> *This book does not project trends; it examines discontinuities.*
> *It does not forecast tomorrow…It asks instead: 'What do we*
> *have to tackle today to make tomorrow?'*
>
> Peter Drucker in the preface to
> *The Age of Discontinuity*, Heinemann, 1969.

Today we are going to summarise the key points of the
week and highlight the key points of strategy:

- Reviewing the week
- Seven thought-starters
- The end, or the beginning

Reviewing the week

We began the week by defining strategy as: *what we want to do,*
what we want our organisation to be and where we want it to go.

Strategy differs from 'tactics' and 'planning' by providing
an organisation with a framework for it to:

- understand its position in the changing marketplace
- move forward with a sense of purpose and urgency
- focus on the key issues of customers and markets,
  and on the skills needed to deliver to those
  customers and markets

Next, we looked at how strategy got bogged down in a
complexity of models, and highlighted the reasons why
these models were unable to stand up to the rigours of the
late 1980s and 1990s:

- Models can't predict the future with any certainty using information and experience from past conditions.
- Models focus on products, markets and resources but not on generating values and capabilities for the future. What companies are good at today may not and probably will not – be what they need to be good at tomorrow.
- Models become preoccupied with maintaining the current position rather than with frameworks for reflection and questioning where to go next.
- Models require an intensity of effort that locks the organisation into set processes and removes the flexibility to adapt and change direction.

On Tuesday we looked at some of the acknowledged strategists whose message focused on:

- being flexible to adapt to the changing environment
- reinventing new ways of attracting and retaining customers
- doing things differently and doing different things to stand out from the pack
- rejecting industry conventions and boundaries, by thinking creatively and acting boldly
- involving everyone within the organisation in the strategy process, because corporate planners hold no monopoly over good ideas
- preparing for strategic change by asking uncomfortable questions about traditional practices and encouraging straight talking rather than 'covering up' or 'saving face'

On Wednesday, we attempted to make sense of our ever-changing environment by looking at SWOT and PEST analyses and the trends that are changing the way we do business. We moved on from an analysis of the past and present by asking the key questions which can help to determine an organisation's future direction:

- What changes are happening in today's markets?
- How well do you think your organisation's current strategy will fit into the future?
- How quickly could your organisation change to take advantage of opportunities and defend against threats?
- In which market areas do you have the best chance of success?
- What is happening to customers' attitudes and demands?
- Will the critical success factors of today hold good for tomorrow?
- What key skills do you need to develop?

On Thursday we looked at the key factor in formulating strategy: strategic thinking; creating problems and setting challenges which take the organisation down a different path from that of the past. This means:

- casting off a risk-averse culture and replacing it with a culture where new ideas are encouraged and positively assessed
- working from the future back to the present, rather than looking forward from the past
- reinventing the organisation where necessary so that individual learning and development are at the heart of strategy, and the rewards for individuals are geared to it

On Friday we took a brief look at the basis of a new strategic approach which integrates organisational developments and goals with the personal values of learning, improvement and employability. The key to success here is the alignment of organisational with personal development tools. Emerging CPD schemes are beginning to provide one way forward. Making learning work for the individual is an important first step – organisational learning will not work without it.

Seven thought-starters

The development of strategy is an art rather than a science, and as such there can really be no set rules. We stress some key factors to help you get started in ensuring that your organisation's strategy stands a chance of success:

1 *Seriously question, if not totally ignore, tradition.* Think outside of the 'box' within which your organisation operates. No organisation can afford to believe that competition or changes will come from solely within its own industry, or that a small firm cannot overturn the largest. Who would have thought – a few years ago – that supermarkets would move into the banking sector in the UK? The opportunities and threats for organisations in the present environment are limited only by an organisation's ability to break industry traditions, conventions and boundaries. This means keeping a sharp eye on surroundings and asking unwelcome questions which can cause conflict.

2 *Involve everyone – follow a top-down and bottom-up approach to strategy.* None of us has a monopoly on

good ideas, and no-one can predict the future with any accuracy. Successful organisations focus on the customer, yet it is most often the people furthest away from the customer who develop strategy. Beware of the seven deadly sins of comfort, complacency, conceit, convention, following fads without strategic purpose, overreliance on experience, and confusing computer-generated data with knowledge.

3 *Avoid 'paralysis by analysis'.* Spending too much time and effort trying to develop the most accurate and detailed picture of today does not enable us to get in position to determine the future, or *make tomorrow*, as Drucker says. Look ahead, but not blindly nor obsessively; remember the saying 'If you keep your eyes on the distant horizon, you may trip over a stone', but don't just look at the stones.

4 *Encourage and foster innovation and creativity throughout the organisation.* Doing something different requires the need for innovation within an organisation. To help foster innovation, an organisation must ensure that risks are allowed and that employees who take them with the goal of improving organisational success are not blamed if they don't work out. Strike a balance between accountability on the one hand and risk on the other. Ensure that staff have an opportunity for development *and* to make their contribution.

5 *Go for balance.* There has to be a balance between getting things done (maintenance) and tackling new things (progress), and a balance between focus on the quarterly returns and an exciting direction for the future.

6 *Embrace conflict as unavoidable in strategic change – and plan to exploit it.* Change can invoke fear; for change to be successful, conflict has to be managed and used to advantage, not ignored.

7 *Remember that strategy never stops.* Organisations can no longer afford to lock themselves into 5- or 10-year strategic plans. Strategy has to be *continually* modified if an organisation is to shape its own direction. The perfect strategy is rarely achieved as a straight line; learning from mistakes will help ensure that it becomes possible.

The end, or the beginning

For some organisations, this week's advice will seem unachievable. We hear cries of 'We can't do that' or 'We don't work like that'. In which case, it probably won't work, because strategy is largely a question of attitude, will and trust.

There are three types of organisation:

1 *The Movers*: organisations which continually change to meet the needs of their environment and constantly innovate to find new ways of delighting their customers and differentiating themselves from the competition. These organisations take a proactive approach to change and innovation, and put learning at the centre of their development.
2 *The Watchers*: organisations that play 'catch-up' with the competition. These organisations wait and see what impact changes in the environment have, and then copy the successes of other organisations. Such organisations will remain in a precarious position by being reactive to change and are more likely to become failures than successes.
3 *The Short-lived*: organisations that do not change and innovate, and lose out.

It is a salutary thought that the average life-span of a small business is 3–5 years, even more eye-popping that for a large one it's about 30 years. A company may be strong (if a household name, it appears part of the permanent landscape), yet it can disappear very quickly. Current success holds very little sway over future success. Strategy does.